# 101 GREAT ANSWERS TO THE SCHOOL TEACHER INTERVIEW QUESTIONS

## DR DHEERAJ MEHROTRA

Copyright © Dr Dheeraj Mehrotra
All Rights Reserved.

This book has been self-published with all reasonable efforts taken to make the material error-free by the author. No part of this book shall be used, reproduced in any manner whatsoever without written permission from the author, except in the case of brief quotations embodied in critical articles and reviews.

The Author of this book is solely responsible and liable for its content including but not limited to the views, representations, descriptions, statements, information, opinions and references ["Content"]. The Content of this book shall not constitute or be construed or deemed to reflect the opinion or expression of the Publisher or Editor. Neither the Publisher nor Editor endorse or approve the Content of this book or guarantee the reliability, accuracy or completeness of the Content published herein and do not make any representations or warranties of any kind, express or implied, including but not limited to the implied warranties of merchantability, fitness for a particular purpose. The Publisher and Editor shall not be liable whatsoever for any errors, omissions, whether such errors or omissions result from negligence, accident, or any other cause or claims for loss or damages of any kind, including without limitation, indirect or consequential loss or damage arising out of use, inability to use, or about the reliability, accuracy or sufficiency of the information contained in this book.

Made with ♥ on the Notion Press Platform
www.notionpress.com

# Contents

# Preface

*The role of a teacher is pivotal in shaping the future of our society, and the journey to becoming an effective educator often begins with a crucial step: the interview. This process can be daunting, as it requires not only a demonstration of one's knowledge and skills but also an ability to convey passion, dedication, and a vision for education. With this understanding, I present **"101 Great Answers to the School Teacher Interview Questions."***

*This book is designed to be a comprehensive guide for aspiring and current teachers preparing for their interviews. It aims to provide the tools, insights, and confidence needed to excel in your interview and secure your desired teaching position. The questions and answers compiled here are based on extensive research, real-life experiences, and feedback from interviewers and interviewees in the education sector.*

*I hope that **"101 Great Answers to the School Teacher Interview Questions"** becomes a valuable resource, empowering you to step into your interview with confidence and clarity. May* *it guide you toward securing the teaching position that will allow you to inspire and nurture the next generation of learners.*

*Sincerely,*

*Dr Dheeraj Mehrotra*

*Author*

"Teachers inspire dreams, ignite curiosity, and instil a love for learning, shaping the future one student at a time with dedication and compassion."

vii

# CHAPTER ONE

# GET SET GO

*Interview Questions with Answers for the*
*Job of School Teacher*

"Teachers are the architects of the future, moulding minds, nurturing potential, and fostering a lifelong love of learning with patience, passion, and purpose."

*1. Why did you decide to become a teacher? Answer: Talk about how much you love teaching, how you want to change your students' lives, and how much you love the subject you teach.*

*2. What is your approach to teaching?*
*Answer: Talk about what you think about education, how you make your classroom welcoming, and how you get students to learn and be interested.*

*3. What do you do to run the classroom?*
*Answer: Talk about how you keep things in order, make sure everyone knows what's expected of them, and control behaviour with positive feedback.*

*4. How do you teach in different ways?*
*Answer: Describe how you change how you teach to fit the needs of students with different learning styles and levels.*

*5. How do you use technology to make your lessons better?*
*Answer: Give examples of digital tools you use, like interactive whiteboards, teaching apps, and online resources.*

*6. Describe a lesson that went well that you gave.*
*Answer: Write down the lesson plan, the goals, the activities you used, and the results, emphasising how engaged and successful the students were.*

*7. How do you measure how well students are doing?*

*Answer: Talk about formative and final tests, how you use rubrics, and how you give students feedback.*

**8. How do you deal with a kid always making a mess?**

*Answer: Talk about ways to help, such as figuring out the reason, following through on behaviour plans, and getting parents and counsellors involved.*

**9. In what ways do you help kids who have special needs?**

*Answer: Talk about Individualized Education Programs (IEPs), differentiating lessons, and working with special education teachers.*

**10. What do you do to get to know your students?**

*Answer: Talk about how you get to know your kids, show empathy, and make the classroom safe for everyone.*

"Teachers ignite curiosity, inspire dreams, and shape character. They transform challenges into opportunities, guiding students toward their fullest potential with unwavering dedication."

*11. How do you get parents involved in their kids' schooling?*
*Answer: Talk about how to keep in touch with parents, have parent-teacher conferences, and include parents in classroom events.*

*12. How do you deal with stress and maintain
your work-life balance?*
*Answer: Talk about how you handle your time,
care for yourself, and decide what to do first.*

*13. How do you keep up with changes and
trends in education?*
*Answer: Talk about taking classes for
professional growth, going to workshops,
reading educational journals, and joining
teacher networks.*

*14. How do you make the classroom a good
place to be?*
*Answer: Talk about using positive feedback,
setting a respectful tone, and making the
classroom feel like a community.*

*15. Tell me about when you had to change how
you taught.*
*Answer: Give an example of how you changed
your methods to fit the needs of a student or
group of students.*

*16. When kids fight, how do you handle it?*
*Answer: Discuss how you handle conflicts,
such as through mediation, active listening,
and encouraging students to empathise with
others.*

*17. How do you use projects in your lessons?*
*Answer: Explain how you set homework rules*

*and give proper homework that builds on what you've learned in class.*

*18. How do you get your kids ready for extensive tests?*
*Answer: Talk about ways to prepare for tests, how to lower test anxiety, and how to teach test-taking techniques.*

*19. How do you use facts to help you teach?*
*Answer: Talk about how you look at test results to see what your students need and then change how you teach them to meet those needs.*

*20. What do you do well as a teacher?*
*Answer: To solve the problem, stress traits like patience, innovation, adaptability, and good communication.*

"Teachers are the architects of futures, crafting knowledge and nurturing minds with patience, passion, and an unwavering belief in each student's potential."

## 21. In what ways do you think you could do better?

Answer: Admit that you need to improve and explain what you are doing, like getting a coach or more training.

*22. What do you do when a parent disagrees with how you teach?*
*Answer: Tell them how you listen to their worries, show proof that your methods work, and look for common ground.*

*23. How do you make your school more diverse and open to everyone?*
*Answer: Share your ideas on including different ideas and tools and make the classroom a place where everyone feels welcome.*

*24. Tell me about a time when someone gave you helpful comments.*
*Answer: Give an example of how you replied positively and the changes you made.*

*25. What do you do to get your kids excited about learning?*
*- Answer: Talk about how excited you are about the subject, how attractive your lesson plans are, and how you encourage students to be curious and explore.*

*26. What do you do to help students who are learning English (ELLs)?*
*- Answer: Talk about tools like visual aids, simplified language, peer help, and individualized lessons.*

*27. How do you make links between subjects in your lessons?*

- *Answer: Give examples of connecting different areas to make learning more valuable and cohesive.*

*28. How do you deal with students from different cultures when you teach?*
*Answer: Talk about what you're doing to accept cultural differences, learn about your students' cultures, and use various materials.*

*29. How do you get kids who don't care about the subject to learn?*
*Answer: Talk about ways to get them to learn, like making the information relevant to their interests, giving them options, and giving them rewards.*

*30. How do you help kids who are intelligent and talented?*
*Answer: Talk about giving students access to more advanced tools, projects they can do independently, and chances to learn more.*

"Teachers are the unseen heroes, quietly nurturing talent and guiding young minds to explore, learn, and achieve beyond their wildest dreams."

## 31. How do you deal with touchy subjects in the classroom?
- Answer: Describe how you plan to make a safe space for discussion, ensure tools are age-appropriate, and treat different points of view respectfully.

### 32. What part does working with other teachers play in your job?

Answer: Talk about how important it is to work together, share tools, and be a part of professional learning communities.

### 33. How do you teach social and emotional learning (SEL) in your school?

- Answer: Name some things that help kids become more self-aware, learn to control themselves, make friends, and make good decisions.

### 34. How do you help your student's mental health and well-being?

- Answer: Talk about spotting signs of sadness, offering support, and encouraging a healthy lifestyle.

### 35. Describe how you work on your career growth.

- Answer: Talk about how you plan to keep learning by attending classes and using new techniques in your classroom.

### 36. How do you make sure that your lessons are engaging?

- Solution: Talk about using different teaching methods, engaging activities, and learning focused on the students.

### 37. What should you do about a kid who is

*behind?*
*- Answer: Describe how you plan to find the*
*issue, offer extra help, and work with parents*
*and experts.*

*38. How do you plan to use the arts in the*
*classroom?*
*- Answer: Talk about adding creative tasks,*
*encouraging artistic expression, and using the*
*arts in all subjects.*

*39. How do you handle a class with a lot of*
*people?*
*Answer: Share ideas for running a classroom*
*well, setting up group work, and giving each*
*student individual attention.*

*40. How do you deal with feedback from*
*parents or coworkers?*
*- Answer: Talk about how you listen without*
*bias, stay professional, and use comments to*
*get better.*

"A great teacher doesn't just teach; they inspire, motivate, and empower students to believe in their own possibilities and reach for greatness."

*41. Please tell me about when you went the extra mile for a kid.*
*Answer: Give an example of a time when you went above and beyond to help a student grow personally or academically.*

*42. What steps do you take to use project-based learning (PBL) in your classroom?*
*Answer: Talk about using real-world projects, student-led research, and connections between different fields.*

*43. What methods do you use to teach kids who have ADHD?*
*- Answer: Talk about techniques like set routines, clear directions, and breaks for movement.*

*44. What kind of formative testing do you use in your class?*
*- Answer: Describe how you use ongoing tests to see how much your students understand and how you change your lessons accordingly.*

*45. How can you ensure every kid in your class is safe?*
*- Answer: Talk about making rules clear, encouraging respect, and dealing with any bullying or unfair treatment.*

*46. How do you keep parents up to date on their child's progress?*
*- Answer: Talk about regular reports, parent-teacher conferences, and using email or apps or other ways to talk to each other.*

*47. How do you teach controversial subjects?*
*- Answer: Explain how you give balanced points of view, promote critical thought, and*

*value different points of view.*

**48. How do you get kids to move around in the classroom?**
*Answer: Include movement breaks, kinesthetic learning tasks, and health promotion.*

**49. Tell me about your experience doing coursework.**
*- Answer: Give examples of how you've changed or created the curriculum to fit the needs and standards of your students.*

**50. What should you do when a kid isn't doing what you want them to?**
*-- Answer: Describe how you plan to find the problem and help, and if needed, involve parents and other pros.*

"Every lesson a teacher imparts is a building block for the future, shaping students' dreams and guiding them toward their highest potential."

*51. What do you do to teach kids who come from low-income families?*
*Answer: Talk about how to understand their problems, give them tools, and make the classroom a place where everyone feels welcome.*

*52. How do you teach kids in the same classroom with different learning methods?*
*Answer: Share ideas for differentiating teaching, using flexible grouping, and offering different ways to learn.*

*53. How do you teach STEM subjects in your classroom?*
*Answer: Talk about how hands-on projects and lessons that combine subjects can help integrate science, technology, engineering, and math.*

*54. How do you get students to be independent and learn independently?*
*- Answer: Talk about giving students choices, encouraging them to think critically, and using inquiry-based learning.*

*55. What can you do when you don't have enough in your classroom?*
*- Answer: Talk about being resourceful, using community resources, and speaking up for the tools and help you need.*

*56. What methods do you use to teach reading and writing?*
*Answer: Talk about phonics, guided reading, literacy centres, and using a variety of books.*

*57. How can you teach kids to think critically?*

*- Answer: Describe how you support people in asking questions, finding solutions, and thinking about things from different points of view.*

*58. How can play-based learning be used in the early years of education?*
*- Answer: Talk about how play can teach ideas, improve social skills, and spark the imagination.*

*59. How do you plan to teach social studies or history?*
*Answer: Talk about using first-hand sources, connecting past events and current problems, and pushing students to think critically.*

*60. How can formative comments help you become a better teacher?*
*- Answer: Describe how you get feedback from students, coworkers, and yourself to keep getting better.*

"Teachers inspire growth, transform lives, and shape
the world with their commitment to education and the
endless potential of their students."

## 61. What do you do when someone cheats in your classroom?

*- Answer: Talk about making standards clear, teaching honesty, and dealing with problems by giving them the right punishments.*

*62. How do you teach about the world in your classes?*
*- Answer: Talk about incorporating lessons on sustainability, learning outside, and encouraging people to take care of the earth.*

*63. How do you help your students understand math?*
*Answer: Talk about using manipulatives, how they can be used in real life, and how they can help kids learn how to solve problems.*

*64. How do you help kids when they are changing things, like when they move up to a new grade?*
*- Answer: Talk about giving information, easing worries, and ensuring that learning keeps going.*

*65. How do you teach your kids to be good digital citizens?*
*- Answer: Describe how you teach digital literacy, online safety, and how to use the internet responsibly.*

*66. How do you deal with kids who don't follow your rules?*
*Answer: Talk about staying calm, talking about the behaviour in private, and setting clear and constant consequences.*

*67. How do you plan to teach people how to write?*

*- Answer: Talk about teaching writing processes, giving comments, and encouraging people to be creative.*

*68. How do you get people from the neighbourhood to come to your class?*
*- Answer: Talk about field trips, inviting guest speakers, and working with neighbourhood groups.*

*69. How do you help your kids improve their social skills?*
*- Answer: Talk about using social stories, role-playing, and group tasks to learn.*

*70. In what ways do you use reflection practice as a teacher?*
*- Answer: Describe how you regularly evaluate your teaching, set goals to improve, and look for chances to grow professionally.*

"A teacher ignites the spark of curiosity and fuels the flamc of lcarning, guiding students towards a brighter, more informed future."

*71. How do you go about teaching other languages?*
*- Answer: Talk about using immersion methods, cultural events, and speaking and writing with others.*

*72. What should you say to a parent who is mad about their kid's grade?*
*- Answer: Talk about how you listen to their worries, show proof of the student's work, and discuss how they can improve.*

*73. How do you teach students about ethics in the classroom?*
*- Answer: Talk about teaching ideals, moral problems, and encouraging people to act ethically.*

*74. How do you teach kids to make plans and follow through?*
*Answer: Talk about using tasks to set goals, keep track of progress, and celebrate successes.*

*75. How can you ensure every kid is paying attention in class?*
*Answer: Talk about using different ways to get people involved, like asking questions, doing group work, and doing interactive tasks.*

*76. How can you help your students be more aware and less stressed in the classroom?*
*Answer: Talk about using mindfulness exercises, calming the space, and showing people how to deal with stress.*

*77. How do you deal with the different religious beliefs of your kids in the classroom?*
*Answer: Talk about how to value different beliefs, include various points of view, and*

*encourage acceptance.*

*78. What do you do when a student doesn't want to do the things being done in class?*
*- Answer: Describe how you plan to understand the reason, offer help, and get people involved.*

*79. How do you use inquiry-based learning in your classroom?*
*- Answer: Discuss how questions can drive learning, encourage exploration, and push students to find solutions.*

*80. How do you help your kids be creative in the classroom?*
*Answer: Talk about giving kids chances to be creative, encouraging innovation, and valuing their unique ideas.*

Teachers' Favourite
Teaching Strategies
That Work
DR. DHEERAJ MEHROTRA

Now @Amazon!

*81. What should you do about a kid who won't
do their work?*
*- Answer: Describe how you figure out the real
problem, inspire them, and give them extra
help.*

*82. How can you teach your kids to be good
internet citizens?*
*Answer: Talk about teaching kids about
internet safety, ethics, and the importance of
leaving digital traces.*

*83. What should you do if a kid is being picked
on?*
*Answer: Talk about how to spot the signs of
bullying, offer support, and implement anti-
bullying rules and programs.*

*84. When you teach, how do you include
science education?*
*- Answer: Talk about doing experiments,
hands-on exercises, and encouraging people to
ask science questions.*

*85. How can you get students to work
together?*
*- Answer: Talk about using group projects,
cooperative learning tasks, and teaching
people how to work together.*

*86. How do you take care of the mental health
needs of your students?*

*Answer: Discuss how to spot signs of concern, offer help, and create a safe space for everyone.*

*87. How do you teach your children to think critically about what they read?*
*- Answer: Describe how you teach students to use media, evaluate sources, and think critically.*

*88. How do you help your kids grow as people and learners?*
*- Answer: Talk about setting high standards, being a guide, and giving each person individualized help.*

*89. How do you teach social studies while also teaching other subjects?*
*Answer: Talk about using first-hand sources, connecting past events and present problems, and encouraging people to get involved in their communities.*

*90. What should you do about a kid not doing well in school?*
*- Answer: Describe how you figure out the problem, give extra help, and, if needed, involve parents and experts.*

www.authordheerajmehrotra.com

91. How can you encourage a growth attitude in your classroom?
- Answer: Talk to your kids about how to encourage them to keep going, how to praise hard work, and how to welcome challenges.

92. What do you do when students in the same school have different ability levels?
- Answer: Talk about differentiating teaching, using flexible grouping, and giving students different learning methods.

93. What ways do you use physical education

*in your lessons?*
*Answer: Talk about getting people to be more active, incorporating movement into lessons, and teaching health education.*

94. *How do you help your kids improve their emotional intelligence?*
*- Answer: Talk about how SEL exercises can help teach self-awareness, self-control, and empathy.*

95. *What should you do about a student always late to class?*
*- Answer: Describe how you will deal with the problem, figure out what caused it, and put plans in place to be more reliable.*

96. *How do you teach kids to be good members of the world?*
*- Answer: Talk about combining global education, promoting cultural understanding, and encouraging people to be socially responsible.*

97. *How do you help kids take care of their physical health?*
*Answer: Talk about encouraging good habits, teaching nutrition, and getting people moving.*

98. *What should you do when a student doesn't follow the rules in the classroom?*
*Answer: Describe how you ensure everyone knows what is expected of them, what will*

*happen if they don't follow the rules, and how you teach respect.*

*99. How do you use technology to help you teach?*
*- Answer: Talk about how to use digital tools and resources online and how to teach others how to do the same.*

*100. What should you do when a student isn't interested in learning?*
*- Answer: Describe how you find the problem, offer help, and use different ways to get people involved.*

*101. How good are you as a teacher for your students?*

*- Answer:*

*It's essential to highlight your strengths, experiences, and commitment to student success.*

*"I believe I am a highly effective teacher for my students, and my experiences and outcomes support this belief. My teaching philosophy centres around fostering a supportive and engaging learning environment where students*

*feel valued and encouraged to reach their full potential.*

*For example, I have implemented various interactive teaching methods and technology integration in my current role to make lessons more engaging and relevant to my students' lives. One of my proudest moments was when my students completed a project-based learning activity that involved community research and presentation skills, demonstrating their understanding and application of the subject matter.*

*Furthermore, I regularly receive positive feedback from students and parents regarding my approachability, enthusiasm, and dedication. My students have consistently shown academic improvement, with many achieving higher test scores and exhibiting greater confidence in their abilities.*

*However, I always look for ways to improve and adapt my teaching strategies. I attend professional development workshops, collaborate with colleagues, and seek feedback to ensure I provide the best possible education for my students.*

*In conclusion, my dedication to student success, innovative teaching methods, and continuous self-improvement make me a strong and effective teacher for my students."*

Exercise

1. Why did you decide to become a teacher?
- A) Because of the high salary
- B) Love for teaching and desire to impact students' lives
- C) Short working hours
- D) Job security
- Answer: B

2. What is your approach to teaching?
- A) Strict discipline
- B) Creating a welcoming environment and engaging students
- C) Following a rigid curriculum
- D) Minimal interaction with students
- Answer: B

3. What do you do to run the classroom?
- A) Ignore misbehavior
- B) Use positive feedback and clear expectations
- C) Punish students frequently
- D) Allow students to do as they please
- Answer: B

4. How do you teach in different ways?
- A) Using the same method for all students
- B) Ignoring students' individual needs
- C) Adapting teaching methods to various learning styles
- D) Only using technology
- Answer: C

5. How do you use technology to make your lessons better?
- A) Avoiding technology
- B) Using digital tools like interactive whiteboards and teaching apps
- C) Only using textbooks
- D) Relying on students to bring their own devices
- Answer: B

6. Describe a lesson that went well that you gave.
- A) Focused solely on lecturing
- B) Included interactive activities and engaged students
- C) Had no clear objectives
- D) Was disorganized
- Answer: B

7. How do you measure how well students are doing?
- A) Only through final exams
- B) Using formative and summative assessments with feedback
- C) Not assessing at all
- D) Only through group projects
- Answer: B

8. How do you deal with a kid always making a mess?
- A) Ignore the behaviour
- B) Provide support and involve parents and counsellors if necessary
- C) Punish the student harshly
- D) Remove the student from class permanently
- Answer: B

9. In what ways do you help kids who have special needs?
- A) Ignore their needs
- B) Use IEPs and collaborate with special education teachers

- C) Treat them the same as other students
- D) Avoid any specialized instruction
- Answer: B

10. How do you get to know your students?
- A) By maintaining distance
- B) Showing empathy and creating a safe environment
- C) Only during parent-teacher meetings
- D) Through exams only
- Answer: B

11. How do you get parents involved in their kids' schooling?
- A) Avoiding contact with parents
- B) Regular communication and involving them in classroom events
- C) Only during emergencies
- D) Never involving parents
- Answer: B

12. How do you deal with stress and maintain your work-life balance?
- A) Ignoring stress
- B) Managing time, self-care, and prioritizing tasks
- C) Overworking
- D) Avoiding any responsibilities
- Answer: B

13. How do you keep up with changes and trends in education?
- A) Ignoring new trends
- B) Attending professional development courses and workshops
- C) Only teaching traditional methods
- D) Avoiding collaboration with peers
- Answer: B

14. How do you make the classroom a good place to be?
- A) Using positive feedback and creating a community atmosphere
- B) Ignoring student interactions
- C) Discouraging communication
- D) Maintaining strict discipline only
- Answer: A

15. Tell me about when you had to change how you taught.
- A) Sticking to one method
- B) Adapting methods to meet student needs
- C) Ignoring student feedback
- D) Teaching the same way regardless of effectiveness
- Answer: B

16. When kids fight, how do you handle it?
- A) Ignoring the conflict
- B) Using mediation and encouraging empathy
- C) Punishing both students severely
- D) Separating the students permanently
- Answer: B

17. How do you use projects in your lessons?
- A) Never assigning projects
- B) Providing guidelines and ensuring relevance to lessons
- C) Only giving exams
- D) Ignoring project-based learning
- Answer: B

18. How do you get your kids ready for extensive tests?
- A) Ignoring test preparation
- B) Using test-taking strategies and reducing anxiety
- C) Only teaching the test content
- D) Avoiding any test preparation
- Answer: B

19. How do you use facts to help you teach?
- A) Ignoring data
- B) Analyzing assessment results to tailor instruction
- C) Only using anecdotal evidence
- D) Avoiding assessment results
- Answer: B

20. What do you do well as a teacher?
- A) Patience, innovation, adaptability, and communication
- B) Only following the curriculum
- C) Strict discipline
- D) Avoiding student engagement
- Answer: A

21. In what ways do you think you could do better?
- A) Denying any need for improvement
- B) Seeking coaching and further training
- C) Ignoring feedback
- D) Avoiding professional development
- Answer: B

22. What do you do when a parent disagrees with how you teach?
- A) Ignoring the parent
- B) Listening to concerns and finding common ground
- C) Arguing with the parent
- D) Changing methods without evidence
- Answer: B

23. How do you make your school more diverse and open to everyone?
- A) Ignoring diversity
- B) Including various perspectives and materials
- C) Only teaching one culture
- D) Discouraging inclusion
- Answer: B

24. Tell me about a time when someone gave you helpful comments.
- A) Ignoring feedback
- B) Responding positively and making changes
- C) Arguing with the feedback giver
- D) Avoiding any response
- Answer: B

25. What do you do to get your kids excited about learning?
- A) Showing enthusiasm and creating engaging lessons
- B) Only giving lectures
- C) Ignoring student interests
- D) Using outdated materials
- Answer: A

26. What do you do to help students who are learning English (ELLs)?
- A) Ignoring their needs
- B) Using visual aids and individualized lessons
- C) Treating them the same as native speakers
- D) Avoiding any exceptional support
- Answer: B

27. How do you make links between subjects in your lessons?
- A) Keeping subjects separate
- B) Connecting different areas for cohesive learning
- C) Only focusing on one subject at a time
- D) Avoiding interdisciplinary connections
- Answer: B

28. How do you deal with students from different cultures when you teach?
- A) Ignoring cultural differences
- B) Accepting and learning about their cultures
- C) Only teaching one culture

- D) Discouraging diversity
- Answer: B

29. How do you get kids who don't care about the subject to learn?
- A) Ignoring their lack of interest
- B) Making the information relevant and giving options
- C) Forcing them to study
- D) Using outdated methods
- Answer: B

30. How do you help kids who are intelligent and talented?
- A) Treating them the same as others
- B) Providing advanced resources and independent projects
- C) Ignoring their needs
- D) Only using basic materials
- Answer: B

# 100 STRATEGIES TO EFFECTIVELY PREPARE FOR AN INTERVIEW FOR THE POSITION OF A TEACHER

*1. Conduct thorough research on the school, including its goal, vision, curriculum, and student demographics.*
*2. Comprehend the Role: Familiarize yourself with the teaching role's precise prerequisites and anticipated responsibilities.*
*3. Familiarize yourself with*

*educational ideas: Acquaint yourself with critical educational theories and understand how they relate to your teaching approach.*

*4. Develop Your Philosophy of Education: Clearly express your educational philosophy.*

*5. Revise Your Resume: Make sure your resume is up-to-date, concise, and customized for the specific job.*

*6. Compile References: Prepare a comprehensive list of professional references.*

*7. Familiarize Yourself with Your Strengths: Be ready to discuss your strengths as an educator.*

*8. Identify Areas for Improvement: Acknowledge your shortcomings and describe the steps you are taking to address them.*

*9. Compile Illustrations: Gather specific instances of your accomplishments and difficulties in teaching.*

*10. Comprehend Classroom Management: Prepare to discuss your tactics for managing the classroom.*

*11. Familiarize Yourself with Common Questions: Foresee and rehearse responses to frequently asked interview questions.*

*12. Familiarize yourself with your teaching approaches: Clearly articulate your preferred teaching methods and explain their efficacy.*

*13. Demonstrate Technological Proficiency: Emphasize your aptitude for incorporating technology in educational settings.*

*14. Emphasize Professional Development: Share any recent experiences related to enhancing professional skills and knowledge.*

*15. Compile a Teaching Portfolio: Gather lesson plans, student work samples, and other pertinent resources.*

*16. Demonstrate Proficiency in Curriculum Development: Be ready to discuss your expertise in designing and developing educational curricula.*

*17. Familiarize yourself with Assessment Strategies: Describe your methods for evaluating student learning and adjusting your teaching.*

*18. Familiarize yourself with Behavioral Questions: Reflect on your approach to managing classroom difficulties and student conduct.*

*19. Comprehend Differentiation: Prepare to articulate how you adapt instruction to meet the needs of students with varying learning styles and abilities.*

*20. Prepare for a Discussion on Collaboration: Share your expertise in collaborating with colleagues, parents, and the community.*

*21. Stay Updated on Current Educational Trends: Keep yourself updated about the most recent developments and patterns in education.*

*22. Formulate Inquiries for the Interviewer: Ensure that you have well-considered queries prepared on the educational institution and the specific role.*

*23. Engage in Active Listening: Demonstrate that you are a focused and receptive listener.*

*24. Dress Professionally: Select suitable clothing that conveys the gravity of the interview.*

*25. Punctuality is Key: It is advisable to come at least 15 minutes before to the scheduled interview time.*

*26. Ensure you have essential documents: Keep duplicates of your curriculum vitae, portfolio, and references readily available.*

*27. Hone Your Introduction: Ensure you have a succinct and self-assured self-introduction ready.*

*28. Maintain a Positive Attitude: Sustain a positive mindset throughout the interview.*

*29. Display Zeal: Exhibit your enthusiasm for instructing and collaborating with students.*

*30. Maintain Composure: Employ relaxation techniques to handle interview nervousness effectively.*

*31. Practice Honesty: Respond to inquiries with complete truthfulness and genuine sincerity.*

*32. Demonstrate Versatility: Be ready to engage in conversations about your capacity to adjust to various teaching situations.*

*33. Comprehend School regulations: Acquaint yourself with prevalent rules and protocols.*

*34. Anticipate Scenario Questions: Contemplate how you would manage particular classroom circumstances.*

*35. Emphasize Student Engagement: Explore techniques for fostering and sustaining students' active involvement and enthusiasm.*

*36. Examine Parental Involvement: Analyze strategies for engaging parents in the educational process.*

*37. Familiarize yourself with the field of special education: Learn about the many strategies and laws related to special education.*

*38. Develop Cultural Competence: Demonstrate respect and comprehension of various cultures and backgrounds.*

*39. Prepare for a Discussion on Inclusion: Describe your approach to fostering an inclusive school climate.*

*40. Familiarize oneself with ELL strategies: Converse about various approaches to instructing individuals learning the English language.*

*41. Anticipate Inquiries Regarding Data: Ensure you are prepared to discuss how you utilize data to guide instructional decisions.*

*42. Extracurricular Involvement: Please include details about participating in extracurricular activities or committees.*

*43. Demonstrate Leadership Abilities: Discuss instances when you have assumed leadership positions.*

*44. Familiarize yourself with State Standards: Acquaint yourself with the educational standards set by your state and understand how you fulfil them.*

*45. Emphasize Proficiency in Communication: Elaborate on your aptitude for effectively communicating with students, parents, and colleagues.*

*46. Comprehend the School's Requirements: Demonstrate your understanding of the distinct demands and difficulties faced by the school.*

*47. Prepare to Engage in a Conversation About Professional Objectives: Articulate your aspirations for your profession's immediate and distant future.*

*48.	Familiarize yourself with Assessment Tools: Acquire knowledge about different assessment tools and understand their usage.*

*49. Demonstrate comprehension of student development by exhibiting expertise in child and adolescent development.*

*50.	Familiarize yourself with Technology Questions: Ensure that you are well-prepared to discuss how you use technology in your teaching methods.*

*51. Examine Project-Based Learning: Share your encounter with project-based learning.*

*52.	Emphasize	Creativity: Demonstrate how you use creativity in your lesson planning and instructional methods.*

*53. Prepare comprehensive responses in anticipation of follow-up inquiries.*

*54. Examine Peer Collaboration: Describe your involvement in collaborating with fellow instructors to enhance instructional practices.*

*55. Understand Your Influence: Be ready to talk about your effect on student learning.*

*56. Comprehend Standardized Testing: Share your encounter with standardized testing and its significance in the field of education.*

*57. Demonstrate Strong Organizational Skills: Emphasize your proficiency in maintaining order and efficiently managing time.*

*58. Prepare for Classroom Environment Discussion: Describe your methods for establishing a constructive and efficient classroom atmosphere.*

*59. Emphasize Notable Instances of Student Achievement: Provide concrete illustrations of student triumphs and elucidate your contribution to their accomplishments.*

*60. Acquire knowledge of prevalent instructional software and tools.*

*61. Prepare for Parent Communication Questions: Explain your methods of parent communication and strategies for engaging them in their child's education.*

*62. Comprehend Ethical Dilemmas: Be ready to engage in conversations on moral predicaments in education and demonstrate your ability to manage them.*

*63. Demonstrate Flexibility: Emphasize your capacity to adjust and thrive in the face of new challenges and shifts in the schooling environment.*

*64. Examine Your Learning Style:*

*Analyze your learning style and its impact on your teaching methods.*

*65. Emphasize Mentorship Experience: Indicate any instances where you have provided guidance and support to fellow educators or students.*

*66. Prepare for Cultural Sensitivity Questions: Explain your methods for promoting cultural sensitivity in your classroom.*

*67. Demonstrate Proficiency in Maintaining Professional limits: Exhibit your ability to comprehend and uphold appropriate professional limits when interacting with students.*

*68. Emphasize Collaboration: Elaborate on your proficiency in collaborating efficiently within a team setting.*

*69. Acquire Proficiency in Classroom Technology: Gain knowledge and expertise in classroom technology and its utilization.*

*70. Elaborate on Continuous Improvement: Describe your methods to enhance your teaching approach consistently.*

*71. Get ready to address conflict resolution questions by being prepared to discuss your methods for resolving problems in the classroom.*

*72. Comprehend Social-Emotional Learning: Elaborate on the significance of social-emotional learning and describe how you integrate it.*

*73. Emphasize Community Engagement: Discuss your participation in the school community and other community initiatives.*

*74. Anticipate professional Goals Inquiries: Ensure a clear understanding of your professional objectives and how this role aligns with them.*

*75. Familiarize yourself with education legislation: Stay informed about the latest education legislation and understand how it affects teaching.*

*76. Demonstrate Problem-Solving Proficiency: Elaborate on your approach to resolving challenges within the classroom and school setting.*

*77. Demonstrate Proficiency in Understanding Diverse Learning Styles: Exhibit your ability to comprehend and cater to various learning styles in your instructional approach.*

*78. Examine Effective Literacy Strategies: Share your approaches to instructing literacy at various grade levels.*

*79. Prepare for Technology Integration Questions: Familiarize yourself with discussing incorporating technology into your instructional practices.*

*80. Examine Student-Centered Learning: Elaborate on your involvement with student-centered learning methodologies.*

*81. Familiarize yourself with classroom routines: Ensure you can converse about your classroom routines and protocols.*

*82. Identify Professional Development Needs: Discuss your specific requirements and intentions for professional growth.*

*83. Exhibit enthusiasm and eagerness for teaching: Display your deep interest and excitement for teaching and collaborating with students.*

*84. Examine Time Management: Emphasize your proficiency in efficiently managing time within a demanding academic setting.*

*85. Get ready to address inquiries about your approach to managing diversity in the classroom.*

*86. Discuss a range of evaluation procedures employed to measure student learning.*

*87. Demonstrate Innovation: Describe any novel educational approaches or initiatives you have introduced.*

*88. Familiarize yourself with Parent-Teacher Conferences: Ensure you are ready to discuss your strategy for engaging in parent-teacher conferences.*

*89. Examine Classroom Technology Management: Describe your approach to managing technology usage in your classroom.*

*90. Familiarize yourself with the school's improvement plans and understand how you may make a meaningful contribution.*

*91. Comprehend Student Motivation: Elaborate on the methods to inspire students to attain their highest potential.*

*92. Demonstrate Leadership Potential: Emphasize any indications of your potential for leadership and your objectives in this area.*

*93. Anticipate Ethical issues: Be prepared to engage in conversations about your approach to resolving ethical issues in the field of education.*

*94. Acquire knowledge about special education needs and understand how to handle them effectively.*

*95. Examine Instructional tactics: Identify and explain your preferred instructional tactics and their effectiveness.*

*96. Exhibit Versatility: Display your ability to adjust and adapt to unfamiliar circumstances quickly.*

*97. Preparing for Multicultural*

*Education Questions: Explain your approach to integrating multicultural education into your teaching methods.*

*98. Comprehend Educational Research: Familiarize yourself with up-to-date educational research and its influence on your professional approach.*

*Emphasize your proficiency in effectively communicating with kids, parents, and colleagues as a critical skill.*

*100. Demonstrate Authenticity: During the interview, present your true self and allow your genuine enthusiasm for teaching to radiate.*

"The heart of a teacher is a beacon of light, guiding students through their journey with patience, dedication, and unwavering belief in their potential."

54

# CHAPTER THREE

# DRESS CODE- A REQUISITE

"Teachers are the architects of future success,
constructing the foundation of knowledge and character
upon which students build their dreams."

## *General Guidelines*
*1. Professional Attire: Choose clothing that reflects a professional image. This typically means business casual attire.*
*2. Comfort and Practicality: Wear comfortable and practical clothes for a teaching environment where you may need to move around a lot.*
*3. Modesty: Avoid clothing that is too tight, short, or revealing.*
*4. Clean and Neat: Ensure your clothes are clean, well-fitting, and in good condition.*


## *Specific Suggestions for Women*
*1. Tops: Blouses, dress shirts, sweaters, and professional tops. Avoid low-cut tops and anything too sheer/ Sarees/ Dupattas per the school culture.*
*2. Bottoms: Dress pants, skirts, and dresses. Skirts and dresses should be knee-length or longer.*
*3. Footwear: Comfortable but professional shoes, such as flats, loafers, or low-heeled shoes. Avoid overly casual footwear like flip-flops or sneakers.*
*4. Accessories: Keep jewellery and accessories*

minimal and professional. Avoid anything too flashy or noisy.

## Specific Suggestions for Men

1. Shirts: Dress shirts, collared shirts, or polo shirts. Ties are optional but can add a professional touch.
2. Pants: Dress pants or khakis. Avoid jeans unless specified otherwise by the school policy.
3. Footwear: Professional shoes such as loafers or dress shoes. Ensure they are polished and in good condition.
4. Accessories: Belts and ties should complement the outfit. Keep accessories like watches and jewellery minimal and professional.

## Seasonal Considerations

1. Summer: Opt for lighter fabrics and short sleeves while maintaining a professional look. Avoid overly casual summer attire like shorts or tank tops.
2. Winter: Layer with sweaters, cardigans, or blazers. Wear appropriate outerwear that maintains a professional appearance.

## School-Specific Policies

1. Uniforms: Some schools may have specific uniforms or colour codes for teachers.
2. Special Days: Be aware of casual Fridays

*or themed dress days and adjust your attire accordingly.*

*3. Cultural Sensitivity: Respect the cultural norms of the school community. This might include considerations for religious dress codes.*

### Practical Tips

*1. Plan Ahead: Choose your outfit the night before to ensure it's clean and ready.*

*2. Comfort: Make sure your shoes are comfortable enough for a full day of teaching.*

*3. Spare Outfit: Keep an extra set of clothes or a jacket at school for emergencies.*

*4. Weather: Dress appropriately for the weather while maintaining professionalism.*

### Avoid

*1. Casual Wear: Avoid overly casual clothing like jeans (unless permitted), t-shirts, and athletic wear.*

*2. Inappropriate Graphics: Avoid clothing with inappropriate graphics, slogans, or logos.*

*3. Overly Trendy Fashion: While being fashionable is okay, avoid overly trendy clothing that may not appear professional.*

*By adhering to these guidelines, teachers can maintain a professional appearance that commands respect and sets a positive example for students.*

"In every lesson, a teacher weaves threads of hope, knowledge, and inspiration, creating a tapestry of possibilities for their students."

EXERCISE

General Guidelines

1. What clothing should teachers wear to reflect a professional image?
- A) Casual attire
- B) Business casual attire
- C) Sportswear
- D) Party wear
- Answer: B) Business casual attire

2. Which of the following should teachers avoid wearing to maintain modesty?
- A) Blouses
- B) Dress shirts
- C) Tight, short, or revealing clothing
- D) Sweaters
- Answer: C) Tight, short, or revealing clothing

3. What is crucial when selecting clothes for a teaching environment?
- A) Fashion trends
- B) Comfort and practicality
- C) Brand names
- D) Color coordination
- Answer: B) Comfort and practicality

4. What is significant about the condition of a teacher's clothes?
- A) They should be expensive
- B) They should be clean and neat
- C) They should be trendy
- D) They should be colourful
- Answer: B) They should be clean and neat

#### Specific Suggestions for Women

5. Which type of tops are recommended for female teachers?
- A) Low-cut tops

- B) Sheer tops
- C) Professional tops like blouses or dress shirts
- D) Tank tops
- Answer: C) Professional tops like blouses or dress shirts

6. What should be the minimum length for skirts and dresses for female teachers?
- A) Above the knee
- B) Knee-length or longer
- C) Mid-thigh
- D) Ankle-length
- Answer: B) Knee-length or longer

7. Which type of footwear should female teachers avoid?
- A) Flats
- B) Loafers
- C) Flip-flops
- D) Low-heeled shoes
- Answer: C) Flip-flops

8. How should female teachers approach jewellery and accessories?
- A) Wear flashy and noisy jewellery
- B) Keep jewellery and accessories minimal and professional
- C) Wear large, statement pieces
- D) Avoid jewellery altogether
- Answer: B) Keep jewellery and accessories minimal and professional

#### Specific Suggestions for Men

9. What type of shirts are recommended for male teachers?
- A) T-shirts
- B) Dress shirts or collared shirts
- C) Tank tops
- D) Casual shirts

- Answer: B) Dress shirts or collared shirts

10. What type of pants should male teachers avoid unless specified by school policy?
- A) Dress pants
- B) Khakis
- C) Jeans
- D) Slacks
- Answer: C) Jeans

11. Which type of footwear is recommended for male teachers?
- A) Sneakers
- B) Flip-flops
- C) Professional shoes like loafers or dress shoes
- D) Sandals
- Answer: C) Professional shoes like loafers or dress shoes

12. How should male teachers handle accessories?
- A) Wear large, flashy watches
- B) Keep accessories like watches and jewellery minimal and professional
- C) Avoid all accessories
- D) Wear multiple rings and bracelets
- Answer: B) Keep accessories like watches and jewellery minimal and professional

#### Seasonal Considerations

13. What should teachers avoid wearing during summer?
- A) Lighter fabrics
- B) Shorts or tank tops
- C) Short sleeves
- D) Breathable materials
- Answer: B) Shorts or tank tops

14. How can teachers maintain a professional appearance in winter?
- A) By wearing casual winter wear

- B) By layering with sweaters, cardigans, or blazers
- C) By wearing heavy boots
- D) By avoiding layers
- Answer: B) By layering with sweaters, cardigans, or blazers

#### School-Specific Policies

15. What should teachers do if their school has specific uniforms or color codes?
- A) Ignore them
- B) Follow them
- C) Create their own dress code
- D) Wear whatever they want
- Answer: B) Follow them

16. What should teachers be aware of regarding special days at school?
- A) Casual Fridays
- B) Themed dress days
- C) Both A and B
- D) None of the above
- Answer: C) Both A and B

17. Why should teachers respect the cultural norms of the school community?
- A) To show cultural sensitivity
- B) To avoid standing out
- C) To follow personal preferences
- D) To comply with legal requirements
- Answer: A) To show cultural sensitivity

#### Practical Tips

18. Why should teachers plan their outfit the night before?
- A) To save time in the morning
- B) To ensure it's clean and ready
- C) To avoid last-minute decisions
- D) All of the above

- Answer: D) All of the above

19. What is a practical tip for footwear for teachers?
- A) Wear stylish but uncomfortable shoes
- B) Wear comfortable shoes suitable for a full day of teaching
- C) Wear shoes that match their outfit
- D) Wear high heels for a professional look
- Answer: B) Wear comfortable shoes suitable for a full day of teaching

20. Why should teachers keep a spare outfit or jacket at school?
- A) For fashion changes
- B) For emergencies
- C) For a change after school activities
- D) For meetings
- Answer: B) For emergencies

21. How should teachers dress considering the weather?
- A) Dress appropriately for the weather while maintaining professionalism
- B) Dress casually
- C) Wear heavy clothes regardless of weather
- D) Follow summer fashion trends
- Answer: A) Dress appropriately for the weather while maintaining professionalism

#### Avoid

22. What type of clothing should teachers avoid to maintain professionalism?
- A) Casual clothing like jeans and t-shirts
- B) Business casual attire
- C) Formal wear
- D) School-specific uniforms
- Answer: A) Casual clothing like jeans and t-shirts

23. What should teachers avoid on their clothing?
- A) Inappropriate graphics, slogans, or logos
- B) Solid colors
- C) School logos
- D) Brand names
- Answer: A) Inappropriate graphics, slogans, or logos

24. Why should teachers avoid overly trendy fashion?
- A) To avoid appearing unprofessional
- B) To blend in with students
- C) To show fashion sense
- D) To stay comfortable
- Answer: A) To avoid appearing unprofessional

#### Professional Attire and Classroom Conduct

25. Why is it important for teachers to wear professional attire?
- A) To command respect
- B) To set a positive example for students
- C) Both A and B
- D) To showcase fashion trends
- Answer: C) Both A and B

26. How can teachers' attire impact their interactions with students?
- A) Professional attire can enhance authority and respect
- B) Casual attire can foster a friendly atmosphere
- C) Overly trendy attire can distract students
- D) Fashionable attire can improve students' focus
- Answer: A) Professional attire can enhance authority and respect

27. What is one way to ensure a professional appearance?
- A) Wear trendy clothes
- B) Ensure clothes are clean and well-fitting
- C) Wear bright, eye-catching colors

- D) Wear high fashion items
- Answer: B) Ensure clothes are clean and well-fitting

28. How can teachers' attire influence their teaching effectiveness?
- A) Professional attire can create a more focused learning environment
- B) Casual attire can make teaching more relaxed
- C) Trendy attire can keep students interested
- D) Bright attire can make lessons more engaging
- Answer: A) Professional attire can create a more focused learning environment

29. What role does comfort play in choosing a teacher's attire?
- A) Comfort is secondary to fashion
- B) Comfortable attire supports effective movement and engagement
- C) Comfort is irrelevant in a professional setting
- D) Comfortable attire is only for informal settings
- Answer: B) Comfortable attire supports effective movement and engagement

30. Why should teachers maintain a balance between professional and practical attire?
- A) To impress colleagues
- B) To ensure they can move and teach effectively
- C) To compete in fashion with students
- D) To follow strict dress codes only
- Answer: B) To ensure they can move and teach effectively

# CHAPTER FOUR

# Top Online Courses for Teachers

*Top Online 50 Courses for Teachers*

*The field of education is continuously evolving, and teachers must stay updated with the latest trends, methodologies, and technologies. Online courses offer an excellent opportunity for teachers to enhance their skills, knowledge, and effectiveness in the classroom. A teacher plays a vital role in shaping young minds, instilling knowledge, and fostering skills essential for future success. They inspire, guide, and support students, creating a foundation for lifelong learning and personal growth. Their impact extends beyond the classroom, influencing students' confidence, values, and career aspirations.*

A teacher is crucial for nurturing students' intellectual and emotional development. They ignite curiosity, promote critical thinking, and build essential life skills. By creating a supportive learning environment, teachers influence students' academic achievements and personal growth, setting the stage for their future success and societal contributions.

*General Teaching Skills*
*1. Foundations of Teaching for Learning (Coursera)*
*2. Understanding Learning Styles (edX)*
*3. The Teacher's Social and Emotional Learning (Coursera)*
*4. Effective Classroom Management (FutureLearn)*
*5. Differentiated Instruction in the Classroom (Udemy)*

*Technology Integration*
*6. Google Certified Educator Level 1 (Google for Education)*
*7. Integrating Technology in the Classroom (edX)*
*8. Teaching with Technology and Inquiry: An Open Course for Teachers (edX)*
*9. Blended Learning Essentials (FutureLearn)*
*10. Using Technology in the Classroom (Udemy)*

*Classroom Management*
*11. Classroom Strategies for Inquiry-Based Learning (Coursera)*
*12. Positive Behavior Management (edX)*
*13. Teaching Character and Creating Positive*

*Classrooms (Coursera)*
*14. Effective Classroom Management Strategies (Udemy)*
*15. Creating a Positive Classroom Environment (FutureLearn)*

*Special Education*
*16. Autism Spectrum Disorder (Coursera)*
*17. Special Needs Education (Alison)*
*18. Inclusive Education: Essential Knowledge for Success (edX)*
*19. Teaching Students with Disabilities (FutureLearn)*
*20. Supporting Children with Difficulties in Reading and Writing (Coursera)*

*Subject-Specific Courses*
*21. Teaching Math: Grades 7-12 (Coursera)*
*22. Science Teaching: Grades 5-8 (edX)*
*23. Teaching English as a Second Language (Udemy)*
*24. History Teaching: Engaging Students in Learning (FutureLearn)*
*25. Teaching Music in the 21$^{st}$ Century (edX)*

*Professional Development*
*26. Teacher Training: Personal Development (Udemy)*
*27. Becoming a Better Teacher: Exploring Professional Development (FutureLearn)*
*28. Professional Development for Early Career Teachers (Coursera)*
*29. Leadership in Educational Settings (edX)*
*30. Continuous Professional Development for Teachers (Alison)*

Teachers play a pivotal role in shaping the future by nurturing curiosity, encouraging critical thinking, and building students' confidence. They create a supportive environment where learners thrive, adapt to diverse needs, and inspire a passion for knowledge. Their influence extends far beyond the classroom, profoundly impacting students' lives and futures.

*Teaching Strategies*
*31.    Understanding    Student    Motivation*
*(Coursera)*

*32. Innovative Teaching: Engaging Students (FutureLearn)*
*33. Learning to Teach Online (Coursera)*
*34. Project-Based Learning for All Classrooms (edX)*
*35. Assessment for Learning (FutureLearn)*

*Educational Psychology*
*36. Introduction to Educational Psychology (Coursera)*
*37. Mindfulness for Educators (edX)*
*38. Understanding Student Behavior (FutureLearn)*
*39. Positive Psychology in Education (Coursera)*
*40. The Science of Learning (edX)*

*Curriculum and Instruction*
*41. Designing Curriculum for Online Learning (Coursera)*
*42. Understanding Curriculum Design (FutureLearn)*
*43. Creating an Effective Literacy Program (edX)*
*44. Curriculum and Instruction for the 21ˢᵗ Century (Coursera)*
*45. Developing a Curriculum (Udemy)*

*Teaching with Diversity*
*46. Culturally Responsive Teaching (Coursera)*
*47. Teaching for Equity and Justice (edX)*
*48. Multicultural Education (FutureLearn)*
*49. Understanding Gender Equity in Education (Coursera)*
*50. Teaching in Diverse Classrooms (edX)*

"Teachers illuminate the path of learning, turning challenges into opportunities and helping students discover their true potential."

# About The Author

Dheeraj Mehrotra, MS, MPhil, PhD (Education Management)., a white and a yellow belt in SIX SIGMA, a Certified NLP Business Diploma holder, is an Educational

Innovator, Author, with expertise in Six Sigma In Education, Academic Audits, Neuro-Linguistic Programming (NLP), Total Quality Management In Education, an Experiential Educator, a CBSE Resource towards School Assessment (SQAA), CCE, JIT, Five S, and KAIZEN. He has authored over 100 books on computer science, AI, digital body language, NLP, quality circles, school management, classroom effectiveness, and safety and security. A former Principal at De Indian Public School, New Delhi, (INDIA), NPS International School, Guwahati, and Education Officer at GEMS, Gurgaon, with ample teaching experience of over Three Decades, he is a certified Trainer for Quality Circles/ TQM in Education and QCI Standards for School Accreditation/ School Audits and Management. He has also been honoured with the President of India's National Teacher Award in 2006 and the Best Science Teacher State Award (By the Ministry of Science and Technology, State of UP), Innovation in Education for his inception of Six Sigma In Education by Education Watch, New Delhi and Education World- Best Teacher Award, BOLT Learner Teacher Award by Air India, 'Innovation in Education Award 2016' by Higher Education Forum (HEF), Gujarat Chapter, among others. He has developed over 150 FREE EDUCATIONAL MOBILE Apps for the Google Play Store exclusively for Teachers, Students, and Parents. This work has been recognised by the LIMCA BOOK OF RECORDS and INDIA BOOK OF RECORDS as the only Indian to draw that feast. As a founder and president of the IoT Society of India, he also promotes Technology Globally. Dr Mehrotra is presently engaged as a PRINCIPAL at KUNWARS GLOBAL SCHOOL, Lucknow, India. He has conducted over 2000 workshops globally on "Excellence In Education" integrated with Total Quality Management and Six Sigma, Technology Integration in Education (TIE), Developing towards being ROCKSTAR TEACHERS, including Cyberspace, Cyber Security, Classroom Management, School Leadership & Management, and Innovative teaching within classrooms via Mind Maps, NLP and Experiential Learning in Academics. He is an active TEDx speaker and can be viewed on the YouTube TEDx channel. As a premium UDEMY Instructor, he has developed over 500 courses and caters to over 8 Lakh students from 180 countries. He can be visited at www.authordheerajmehrotra.com